LIFE in the Future

VIRTUAL REALITY

Holly Cefrey

HIGH
interest
books

Children's Press®
A Division of Scholastic Inc.
New York / Toronto / London / Auckland / Sydney
Mexico City / New Delhi / Hong Kong
Danbury, Connecticut

Book Design: Christopher Logan
Contributing Editor: Matthew Pitt

Photo Credits: Cover © Brandtner & Staedeli/Corbis; pp. 4, 10 (bottom), 18
© Bettmann/Corbis; p. 7 © C. Moore/Corbis; pp. 8, 41 © Hulton/Archive/Getty
Images; p. 10 (top) © Underwood & Underwood/Corbis; pp. 13, 25 © Roger
Ressmeyer/Corbis; p. 17 © Neal Preston/Corbis; p. 21 (computer illustration)
by Christopher Logan; p. 22 © Museum of Flight/Corbis; p. 26 © Globe Photos
Inc.; p. 29 © Michael Busselle/Corbis; p. 31 © Steve Raymer/Corbis; p. 33
© AFP/Corbis; p. 34 © Douglas Kirkland/Corbis; p. 37 © Michael Pole/Corbis

Library of Congress Cataloging-in-Publication Data

Cefrey, Holly.
  Virtual reality / Holly Cefrey.
      p. cm. — (Life in the future)
Summary: Introduces virtual reality, exploring the technology involved
and looking toward what the future might bring as VR is used more widely
in entertainment, education, science and medicine.
  ISBN 0-516-23919-8 (lib. bdg.)— ISBN 0-516-24010-2 (pbk.)
  1. Virtual reality—Juvenile literature. 2. Computer
simulation—Juvenile literature. [1. Virtual reality. 2. Computer
simulation.] I. Title. II. Series.
  QA76.9.V5 C44 2002
  006—dc21
                                    2002001905

CONTENTS

3-D glasses may have been flimsy, but the excitement they provided was no cheap thrill.

In 1952, audiences flocked to theaters to view an unusual film. It was an adventure movie called *Bwana Devil*. Its filmmakers promised to put "a lion in your lap." They weren't kidding! Before *Bwana Devil* began, each spectator was given a pair of glasses. The glasses were made of cheap plastic and flimsy paper. One lens was green. The other was red. When the house lights dimmed, the screen seemed to come alive. The film's villains were two ferocious lions. As the lions prowled on-screen, they seemed as though they were about to jump out of the film and into the laps of moviegoers. This was the first, full-length, three-dimensional (3-D) film. The 3-D glasses given to the audience made the flat-screen images seem to have depth. It was thrilling. The audience knew the lions weren't real. Yet they seemed so close....

These days, we can use computers to create lifelike 3-D images. These images are far more thrilling than those of the 3-D movies of the past. Using computers to make lifelike, artificial objects is called virtual reality (VR).

Users of VR believe they are seeing, hearing, and even touching things that are not really there. Virtual reality can transform an ordinary room into Mount Everest. Using virtual reality, you could shrink to the size of a bug. You could play with creatures that do not exist. And you could do all these things within minutes of each other.

VR can be used for more than just entertainment. It can be used to pull off astounding feats in the worlds of medicine, science, and education. In this book, you'll be given a "virtual tour" of how virtual reality works. You'll even get a glimpse into how its future might someday shape yours.

Virtual reality can bring the most amazing sensations right into your family room.

Popular toys like the View-Master gave kids the chance to see flat images come alive.

CHAPTER ONE

Understanding Virtual Reality

In order to understand virtual reality, you need to understand how your mind and eyes work together to view images. Here's an easy experiment. Hold your forefinger about six inches in front of your face. Look at the finger with your left eye closed. Now, look at it with your right eye closed. Switch quickly from one eye to the other. Even though you're holding your finger still, the image seems to pop from left to right. Your left eye is seeing a slightly different image from your right. But when you look at your finger with both eyes, your brain instantly puts both images together.

Objects all around you are three dimensional. However, the images of those objects are not. When you look at a car parked on the street, it has depth. But if you look at a picture of that car, it's flat. To create a 3-D image of the car, virtual reality systems would display two flat images of the same car. The system triggers your mind into combining the two images. This combination creates an image that appears to have depth. Being able to see things in 3-D is also called stereoscopic vision.

Stereoscopes are devices that give depth to flat images. The inset illustration above shows a stereoscope from 1861.

A virtual reality program generates two images on separate display screens. The images are similar, but slightly different. Viewers of virtual reality look at the two flat images. When they do, the images come together in a way that tricks the mind. To the viewers' eyes, these images appear to have depth.

PROGRAMMING VIRTUAL REALITY

Virtual reality programs can create entire virtual environments. They follow human movement and adjust the images to match up. Let's say you were looking at a virtual image of a monkey in a tree. But you can't quite "see" the monkey. The virtual tree leaves are hiding the monkey from your view. A virtual reality program could sense if you moved your head to get a better view. It would then give you a better view of the monkey. You can move in a virtual reality environment, and that environment will seem to move with you. It interacts with your movements, almost instantly.

To achieve this amazing effect, virtual reality programs use many tools. These tools include graphics and animation. Graphics and animation are used to create simulation. A simulation is a copy of something, such as an environment.

Sound can also be used to enhance a virtual environment. If you were on a virtual beach, you could "see" the waves crashing against golden sand. As you stepped closer to the virtual ocean, the sound of the virtual waves would grow louder, too!

Virtual Computer Systems

Three main computer systems provide virtual environments: HMD, BOOM, and CAVE.

HMD
(Head Mounted Display)

The HMD is basically a helmet. The user sees computer images inside of the helmet. The images appear on two small screens. These screens can be

VR demonstrations can be amazing affairs. At this one, the VR user picks up a virtual rock and takes a virtual tour of a Martian landscape.

as small as 1 to 2 inches wide (2.5 to 5 centimeters). Each eye views a slightly different image of the same thing. Your brain puts the two images together. Because of this, your eyes perceive the two images to look like one three-dimensional object.

To make the experience seem more real, tracking devices and headphones are part of the HMD. Tracking devices allow the computer to know how, when, and where you move. The computer matches its images to your movement. Headphones play sounds that make the virtual environment seem real.

BOOM
(Binocular Omni-Orientation Monitor)
The BOOM is shaped like a box. Display screens are inside of it. Users look into the BOOM to see different virtual environments. They move through the virtual world by moving an arm that's attached to the BOOM. Each time the user moves the arm, the arm sends signals to the BOOM. These movements tell the BOOM which images to display.

CAVE
(Cave Automatic Virtual Environment)

A CAVE system uses an entire room to work its virtual magic. Display screens surround the room. When the program begins, computer images are projected across the walls and floor. CAVE users wear special glasses that make the images seem to have depth. While inside the CAVE, you're free to walk around. The CAVE tracks your movements through the glasses. Images are quickly adjusted to match your position. A great thing about the CAVE is that your friends can join you. You could all experience one virtual world at the same time. One user would be the active viewer. That viewer controls which direction the images go in. When the active viewer takes a step forward, the images change for the others, too!

VIRTUAL ACCESSORIES

Different gadgets have been created to enhance the virtual experience. These accessories include gloves and handheld devices.

Users can wear special gloves that allow virtual objects to be moved. The computer is able to match hand movements and gestures. Say you spotted a virtual stone that you wanted to pick up. As your gloved hand moved toward the virtual stone, the image would change to match your movement.

Some gloves can even make you feel like you're holding a virtual object. As you close your hand around the virtual object, these special gloves push slightly against your fingers. When this pressure hits your fingers, you feel like you're touching the surface of a real object! Gadgets that imitate our sense of touch in a virtual environment are called haptic accessories.

Handheld devices can also help users navigate through virtual worlds. There are special

Why is this man smiling? Could it be that his special glove makes him feel like he's holding an apple?

mice, trackballs, and wands. These gadgets have tracking devices inside of them. The tracking devices instruct the computer which images to display on their screens.

Virtual History

Virtual reality history grew alongside advances in computer technology. In the late 1950s, computers were huge, power-gobbling machines. Most were used for crunching numbers. People soon realized that the potential for computers was virtually limitless.

GREAT STRIDES

A 1956 project called Sensorama was the world's introduction to virtual reality. Designed by Morton Helwig, Sensorama looked like an arcade game. The machine displayed a 3-D film of a motorcycle ride through Manhattan. Viewers sat down and gripped a pair of handlebars. As the movie played, viewers felt quick gusts of air on their faces. They could smell

The earliest computers were enormous. Yet they didn't have a fraction of the features that today's VR goggles possess.

exhaust fumes that Helwig had pumped in. When virtual motorists passed a pizza parlor in the film, Sensorama sent odors of tomato sauce and cheese into the air.

In 1962, scientist Ivan Sutherland invented a program called Sketchpad. Using Sketchpad, artists and designers could draw images directly onto a computer screen. They drew images using a handheld lightpen created by Sutherland. For the first time, visual images could be stored in a computer's memory banks. Designers could then return to that image the next time they switched the computer on.

THE FIRST VIRTUAL ENVIRONMENT

Sketchpad made it possible for computers to work with graphics and numbers. Yet Sutherland's work was far from finished. Despite Sketchpad's success, the computer images still looked flat. Sutherland wanted to create images with depth. In 1965, he developed the world's first virtual environment. He called it the Ultimate

Display. The Ultimate Display showed viewers a simple virtual room. This virtual room contained four walls. Each wall had a direction: north, south, east, and west. A person would "enter" the virtual room from a door on the west wall. Wearing an HMD, the viewer could turn and look out virtual windows on the other three walls.

BETTER TOOLS

As computers became more powerful, they took on new and exciting roles. Virtual programs were designed to train military and commercial pilots. Pilots learned to fly by doing flight simulations. Wearing HMDs, they sat in fake cockpits. The pilots felt like they were really flying through clouds and over mountains.

Graphics became sharper and more realistic in the 1980s. At the same time, computers were built with more memory to hold more complex images.

Airplane designers, for example, were able to view 3-D models of their designs and plans. The designers could easily make changes to their plans by altering their virtual creations. And their changes didn't cost a dime!

Data gloves were also invented in the 1980s. Data gloves and HMDs aided the space program at the National Aeronautics and Space Administration (NASA). Using data gloves and HMDs, researchers could control space station robots from a distance. Astronauts also used the devices to train for dangerous space walks.

The new technology wasn't used only for scientific purposes. Several composers used data gloves to make music. Special programs could link human hand gestures to computerized musical instruments. The Mattel toy company made their own version—the PowerGlove. It was used in virtual reality video games.

VR flight simulators provide new pilots with valuable training before they take to the skies.

MARCHING ON

In 1984, scientists Scott Fisher and Mike McGreevy worked at Moffett Field, California, for NASA's Ames Research Center. There, they built a system called Virtual Interface Environmental Workstation, or VIEW. The first model was made from a motorcycle helmet. It contained two inexpensive Sony Watchman TVs. This model proved that virtual systems didn't need to be costly.

Later virtual reality advances include the Virtual Reality Responsive Workbench. Virtual workbenches allow groups of users to interact with the same virtual environment at the same time. Each user wears special glasses. They sit or stand around a large workbench. Virtual images hover above the workbench. The images can be manipulated by using gestures and voice commands.

With virtual reality, thousands of exciting worlds are right at your fingertips.

CHAPTER THREE

Virtual Reality in the Real World

The popularity of virtual reality has taken off. This technology can be used to design things, teach lessons—and to just have fun.

Entertainment

Hollywood is already working with virtual reality technology. A few filmmakers have made movies using virtual "actors." However, when these virtual actors move and speak, the illusion ends. The human face and body is extremely complex. Computer images have trouble showing the range of human motions and emotions.

○ TECH TALK

The film *Gladiator* used 50,000 virtual actors. Computer-generated spectators filled in the scene in the Colosseum. They looked convincing because they weren't shown close up.

On screen, virtual actors do not seem to move in a natural way. However, a company called LifeFX recently unveiled a stunning success. They've created a digital, elderly woman whose expressions and movements are very convincing. To get this effect, LifeFX had to program each layer of "her" virtual body—from skin to bones. It's an exciting breakthrough. But the cost is far too high for Hollywood right now. Still, using virtual actors would have a few advantages. For one thing, they would never forget their lines!

Education

Most schools cannot afford virtual reality systems. But some students are beginning to learn from VR programs. Using these programs, students can dissect virtual frogs in their biology class. They can travel through the streets of virtual Mexico for a Spanish-class field trip. They can even explore a virtual Stonehenge. Students could roam around

Some students have used VR technology to see the other side of the world — without leaving the classroom!

the rocks that make up this magnificent landmark in England. They can even explore Stonehenge when it was first built. Imagine watching this historic site form before your very eyes.

Design

Designers and engineers use virtual reality systems to see how their ideas come to life. For instance, architects can "stand" in the middle of one of their virtual houses or buildings. This way, they get a better feel for how their work might look. They can also examine the design, to see if it might have any potential flaws in structure.

Science and Medicine

Virtual reality helps scientists observe and analyze difficult subjects. Many research subjects, such as molecules, are hard to see. Virtual reality can take something as small as a molecule and blow it up to the size of a basketball.

Virtual reality is being used to help treat patients and train doctors. Some programs ease patients' suffering during painful procedures. Some burn centers are trying out these programs. The centers place their burn victims into pleasing virtual environments while their patients wounds are being treated. Pleasing images of virtual sunsets and lush forests may help distract patients from their pain.

Some doctors practice surgery on virtual patients. They use wands that serve as virtual scalpels, or surgical knives. The doctors operate on virtual body parts, such as the brain. This extra practice can be a lifesaver when it's time to perform a real operation.

Physicians are hoping that a pleasing virtual environment might ease the suffering of burn victims.

Training

Some corporations use virtual reality to measure their employees' skills. For example, BP Amoco, an oil and gas supplier, uses a virtual oil delivery truck to train drivers. Unexpected challenges—such as a virtual deer leaping across the virtual road—test a driver's reaction. The experience is videotaped. Later, both the driver and the instructor can review the performance.

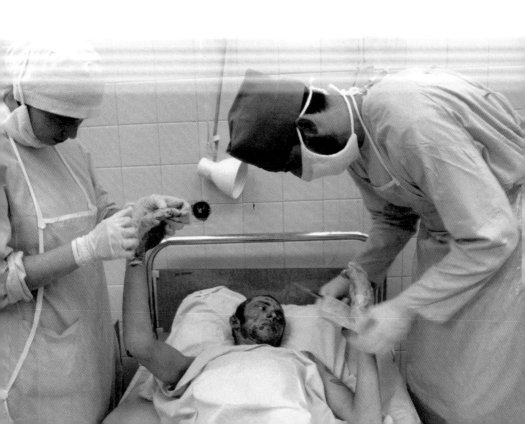

The military is a big believer in the use of virtual reality technology. Some soldiers receive part of their training inside virtual tanks. Inside the virtual tanks, the officers train in realistic combat operations. They learn how to react quickly. Military leaders believe that simulated combat can teach important skills. These skills could come in handy if the soldiers are ever in a real war.

The U.S. Army uses a stairstepper to enhance virtual training. A soldier wears an HMD unit. He or she climbs up on the stairstepper. Virtual battlefield scenes begin to play on the two screens in the soldier's HMD. As the battle unfolds, computers measure the intensity and speed of the soldier's movements. The stairstepper becomes easier or harder to climb depending on the soldier's responses.

Even the military is taking aim at VR technology. Soldiers are receiving some of their training inside virtual tanks and aircraft.

TECH TALK

Developers in Georgia are working on a very special data glove. The glove will allow doctors to virtually feel cancer tumors. Doctors won't even have to be in the same room as their patients. By being able to virtually determine the tumor's size and texture, the doctors will be able to prescribe real treatment.

VR creates a lot of smiles and laughter. Yet if viewers use a system for too long, they could be in for some real pain.

Virtual Future

As fantastic as virtual reality is, some system problems have caused concern. Researchers are working to solve and overcome these problems.

HEALTH

In Scotland, a University of Edinburgh study found that HMDs could cause health problems. VR users frequently experience eyestrain. They may also suffer from blurred vision. Placing the displays farther from the eyes can help. Users are also encouraged to occasionally look away from the screen. This allows the eyes to blink, rest, and readjust to the real world. This simple step may help a VR user's health in the long run.

Some virtual experiences also cause nausea and dizziness. This may lead to seizures. Seizures are caused when the brain becomes disoriented. To be disoriented means to lose track of time and place. People are urged to rest after using virtual systems.

Sometimes, the illusions of virtual reality are *too* convincing. Users who get swept up in VR have a lot of fun. However, they may forget about objects in the real world. HMD users may trip over real objects around them as they're moving about.

Another concern is the weight of some HMDs. Some HMDs weigh several pounds. This added weight can stress out the neck and strain the spine.

FUNCTIONAL ISSUES

Tracking systems must relay information quickly to the computer. The computer must then adjust its images to fit the new information. The VR user must receive these new images almost instantly. This quick exchange makes a virtual reality experience smooth and believable. Sometimes, the lapse between human action and computer adjustment is too long. These

The new technology may someday make a day at the office feel like a day at the beach.

lapses in computer images are known as lag. If lag time is too long, the VR experience will feel choppy.

Another issue is matching real world sensations with those of the virtual world. Let's say you're walking along a virtual ocean coastline. In order for this coastline to seem real, you'd need to feel many sensations. Your feet would need to feel sand, not a carpeted floor. You'd expect to smell salt water in the air. Maybe you would want to enjoy a cool scoop of ice cream. Right now, however, some human senses are too complex to copy. VR programmers have not been

able to imitate taste and smell. They've only begun to work on the sense of touch. Until all your senses are pulled into the virtual experience, VR won't quite measure up to real life.

THE NEAR FUTURE

New VR systems, programs, and accessories are being unveiled each day. Organizations like NASA, Intel, Boeing, and IBM are leading the way. Universities are also making virtual reality come to life.

Walt Disney's Magic Kingdom® in Orlando, Florida, is getting into the act, too. Disney is developing virtual reality games. These games will feature famous Disney characters. The characters will be able to interact with you.

Museums across the country are hoping to develop virtual systems of their own. These systems will be able to anticipate the needs of each paying customer. Getting bored with a painting? The system would be able to sense this, and move you to a different exhibit. Want more information on a sculpture? The computer would instantly tell you an extra, exciting tidbit.

Developers are working on virtual offices, homes, and classrooms. These environments will be internationally accessible. Someone from Japan might be able to virtually visit your geometry class. Maybe your virtual visitor could even help you figure out the area of an isosceles triangle.

Educational software developers are combining important textbook information with fun virtual activities. For example, one group is developing a system that would allow students to virtually shrink down to the size of a cell. The students would then "float" through the systems of the human body.

NASA's Ames Research Center is developing more surgery software that will be used to instruct doctors. One program will teach doctors to reconstruct skull and face bones. Patients with severe face and head damage will benefit from this use of VR. Virtual skin can be placed back on the virtual head to show how the patient will look after the surgery. Doctors can see results before even touching their patients.

Therapists hope to use virtual environments to cure phobias. A phobia is a fear of something. VR could slowly expose a phobic person to a virtual version of their fear. Someone who fears heights might stand on the second floor of a virtual building. Once he or she felt comfortable, the virtual height would increase. Over time, the patient would conquer this fear.

Another project is a virtual guardian for the home. Trackers would be placed inside of a family's house. These trackers would constantly report information about the family to a computer. The trackers could monitor the activities of children in the house. They could warn parents if they sense the children getting into danger.

● *Virtual reality has hit the ground running. No one knows for sure just what heights VR may drive us to in the future.*

FAR INTO THE FUTURE

The future of virtual reality is only limited by our imagination. Someday, we may virtually visit other people in their homes. Perhaps we'll take entire vacations in giant virtual complexes. Children might be able to create things with virtual putty.

This technology may make the unreal—from walks on Mars to time travel—possible. Virtual worlds may all belong in the realm of fantasy. Yet the excitement they can generate is very real.

artificial false; not real

Binocular Omni-Orientation Monitor (BOOM)
a boxed display screen that serves as
a virtual environment

Cave Automatic Virtual Environment (CAVE)
a virtual environment in which images are
projected onto walls and the floor of a cubicle

disoriented to have become confused and
experienced a loss of time and place

graphics realistic images that are generated
by computer

Head Mounted Display (HMD) a device shaped
like a helmet that provides virtual
environment experiences

haptic accessories devices that simulate force or
weight in the virtual world

stereoscopic vision three-dimensional vision

three-dimensional (3-D) having or seeming to have depth

trackers devices that report the position and movement of humans in the real world to computers providing the virtual world

virtual environment an artificial world created by computers

virtual reality an artificial, 3-D environment created by computers

Baker, Christopher W. *Virtual Reality: Experiencing Illusion*. Brookfield, CT: Millbrook Press, 2000.

Jefferis, David, and Mat Irvine. *Cyberspace: Virtual Reality and the World Wide Web*. New York: Crabtree Publishing Company, 1999.

Jortberg, Charles A. *Virtual Reality & Beyond*. Edino, MN: ABDO Publishing Company, 1997.

Pascoe, Elaine. *Virtual Reality: Beyond the Looking Glass*. Farmington Hills, MI: Gale Group, 1997.

Organizations

Computer Learning Foundation
P.O. Box 60007
Palo Alto, CA 94306-0007
(408) 720-8898
www.computerlearning.org

World Kids Network, Incorporated
c/o WAN 2700 NE Andersen Road, #D-32
Vancouver, WA 98661
(360) 247-4WKN

Web Sites

Kidsware Adventures: Play a Drum Set
www.kidsware.com/drumset.html

Hidden New York
www.pbs.org/wnet/newyork/hidden/index.html

PBS—Cool Science
www.pbs.org/safarchive/5_cool/5_cool.html

ABOUT THE AUTHOR

Holly Cefrey is a freelance writer. She is a member of the Authors Guild and the Society of Children's Book Writers and Illustrators.